This Collection of Woeful Poems Was Found in a Notebook at the Bottom of My High School Locker

KIMBERLY LIGHTEN

authorHOUSE®

AuthorHouse™
1663 Liberty Drive
Bloomington, IN 47403
www.authorhouse.com
Phone: 1-800-839-8640

Published by AuthorHouse   09/24/2011

ISBN: 978-1-4567-4162-4 (sc)
ISBN: 978-1-4685-6470-9 (e)

Library of Congress Control Number: 2011903740

CONTENTS

SELF

Out of the darkness and into the light …

FOREWORD

"LIFE AND DEATH" was scrawled in dark-inked, capital letters across the top of the first page. "How did this notebook get in my locker?" I questioned to myself. It was the end of the school year, and I was cleaning out my locker when I came across this black spiral notebook filled with poetry. Since I didn't have any summer plans, I spent my free time reading and later publishing this former student's work.

—Anonymous

LIFE AND DEATH

LIFE INTO DEATH

They sat across the land.
Life said, you will live, Death.
Nothing needs to die,
everything should live.
Death said nothing.
Time passed slowly.
Death said, you will die, Life.
Nothing needs to live,
everything needs to die.
Life said, yes, I will die.
Life was happy to die.
Death was glad it did.
Life began to laugh merrily,
while Death stayed solemn,
preparing to make life into death.

DEATH: PART ONE

Face the fact.

When the time comes, it comes.

DEATH: PART TWO

You are invited to my funeral,
because my life has been completed.

LIFE: PART ONE

Life is like an airport terminal crowded with people.

They push and shove to make their departing flights.

I dodge and cut to just make it through.

So I can be on my merry way.

LIFE: PART TWO

Life is like a baby bird,
with wings that have not yet unraveled.
She tries to fly like her mother,
but she cannot yet travel.
She spreads her wings,
then flaps and flutters until she flies one inch.
She begins to fall,
downward and downward,
until she lands in a ditch.

LIFE: PART THREE

Life is like a camping trip, which should go as planned.

But goes awry,

when your tent is damaged and food is spoiled.

On the side, there is a lake; you can fish for food.

But who knows what's in it?

You'll probably get a moldy sneaker for lunch.

And somehow,

you camped where the bears seem to roam.

So all you end up with is a long walk home.

ISSUES

HERSTORY

Her naked, brown body trembled,
as her master unbuckled his pants.
She thought of escaping to see her family,
who fell upon the hands of other slave owners.
The white man finished undressing,
until only his nude flesh showed.
She whimpered,
but the look in his porcelain blue eyes
made her keep quiet.
He forced her to experience something she never knew.
Her mind traveled away from this horrid scene,
but her body stayed.

RELIGION IS ETERNITY

I have tasted it all,

sampling a bit from each tray of life.

I have discovered plenty.

Oh, do not be amazed,

age plays nobody's role,

but death does.

We try hard to please Him,

or is it Her?

We do not know.

But we try so hard, and I do not know why.

TRUE ANIMALS

I live among the animals
that roam the streets at night.
They search for food,
but its discovery stays unknown.
They dodge away from people,
who come to hurt them.
They trust no one,
not even me.
These animals take me with them,
in my mind.
Other animals I know that roam the streets at night,
I disagree with them.
They burglarize homes, rape women and men,
and kill others to please themselves.
I follow in the footsteps of animals,
true animals.

SIGHTED RACISM

Racism has been placed before my eyes—
blindness in my sight.
If this vision is broken,
I will then see the light.
So much to see,
so much to hear,
does it really matter?
What if the white girl fell first,
and the black girl watched in laughter?

UNACKNOWLEDGED RAPE

I saw the shadowy figure come into my view.
He strayed closer to me,
darting his ebony black eyes at my perplexed face.
I began to run intensely.
He followed me through the empty streets,
until I fell limp.
My tearful eyes tried to search for answers
to clustered questions in his nervous eyes,
but the scene broke.

BREATHING DANGEROUSLY

Strolling down the road,

I looked at the once-blue but now-black sky.

Then I inhaled the putrid stench of the air.

Finally, I remembered how we destroy our atmosphere daily.

Why ruin what we need?

DANGERS THAT THREATEN OUR NATION

Racism

Homelessness

Neglect of the Mentally Ill

Animal Cruelty

Politicians

WATCHING

CHOICES

It was so old and horrifying of a house to be seen.

How could someone so young,

so beautiful live there?

Were those dirty little creatures her friends?

I asked her how she could live like this,

in such a large city filled with wonderful opportunities?

She paused.

Then she responded in a weak voice,

"This city is also filled with deep holes."

A MYSTICAL PRAYER

I run through the dark, rainy Paris streets,

in search of my beloved husband.

At last, I run into his embracing arms,

his lips smothered me with kisses.

He fell short of breath,

falling to the cold, wet concrete.

He died.

Pneumonia took him away.

A crowd of people began to surround us.

They cried more tears than I did.

They took his body away from me.

They buried him next to a bridge that foggy night.

I laid upon his grave

the heart pendant necklace he gave me.

A carriage pulled up next to me,

inside a mysterious gentleman.

He pulled me in at gunpoint.

How dare a man attempt murder upon a recent widow?

He asked me to marry him.

I shook my head.

He fluttered kisses at me.

I reached for his black pistol

and shot him in his greedy heart.

I hurried out of the carriage.

Now I see the light.

Was heaven letting me in, or was hell letting me out?

PEOPLE

I heard the voices of a man and a woman around the corner.

One voice in such pain and agony, that I forced myself to see the situation.

I tiptoed around the corner and peered through the bushes lined against the cement wall.

Then the sound of exploding bullets rang in my ears.

I began to run intensely,

but I went nowhere.

Then she came around the corner,

running toward me,

waving the deadly weapon in her right hand,

as the street audience watched for her next move.

She pushed me out of her way against the hard concrete wall.

I fell down to the ashen ground,

lying there unspoken and blinded by violence.

SHE WEPT BITTERLY

Her chocolate brown eyes filled with tears,
making her fragile face crinkle.
She blew her nose with a tissue,
as I tried to find out why she wept bitterly.
She noticed my questionable eyes,
and tried to respond.
Her lips formed a word, but nothing came out.
Her eyes wandered down to the ground,
where all of her tears fell.
I knew of her sadness by her facial expressions.
But I never knew why she wept bitterly.

THE MAN WHO STANDS
ON THE CORNER EVERY DAY

He stands on the corner every day,

unless the police pick him up.

I wanted to help him and other homeless people,

but my situation remains the same as his—

homeless.

We built a fire last night to keep warm,

while watching poor people with homes pass by

and look away from us.

It brings tears of joy to my eyes to say,

I love the man who stands on the corner every day.

FEMME FATALE ATTRACTION

She strolled across the runway,

tossing her vermilion red hair over her shoulders.

Her long, shapely legs strode in a smooth movement,

while her curved hips swayed with rhythm.

She moved her arms gracefully,

like a ballerina in motion.

Then she smiled innocently,

not knowing what a commotion she had caused.

THE MYSTERIOUS WOMAN

She walked into the room,
jangling her silver, charmed bracelet.
Immediately, she caught everyone's attention.
She mesmerized them with her unique beauty.
Her long, black hair swept away
from her dark-skinned face kept them guessing.
The ivory lace dress held tightly
to her fully curved figure.
Jealousy raged among the women,
while she laughed with their men.
No one knew the name of the girl,
who possessed such loveliness,
but no one saw her after that night.

STUPIDITY

The rich woman showed off her sparkling diamonds,
and her long mink coat to her friends.
She paraded around like a little girl in a new dress,
swirling the coat about her.
Her colleagues praised her
for making an excellent choice in winter apparel.
I sat silently on the porch across the street,
shaking my head in disbelief.
I thought of how much a mistake that woman made.
Is her mind not aware of what crime made that fur?
I started to cry,
not only for the animals,
but for the ignorance of the woman.

MOTHER, MOTHER

Her mother slapped her small, pale face
and ordered her to clean her room.
The girl began to cry,
but her mother threatened her not to
or punishment awaited her.
The girl ran to her room.
Her mother tortured her every night
with cruelness only she possessed.
I wanted this crisis to end.
I ran up to the little girl's window
and tapped on the glass.
The innocent face came into my view.
Then I saw the flame red streaks across her face.
She unlatched the lock of the window
and began to open it slowly.

Then her mother whisked open the wooden door
and began to yell at her child.
I stayed unnoticed
until I pushed open the window and climbed in,
which left the mother in shock.
I looked into the girl's swollen eyes, redden with fear,
and pulled her frail body behind me.
I started to argue with the mother,
until her eyes redden like her daughter's eyes.
She became aware of the fact
of how severely she had victimized her only child.
We all sat down on the neatly made bed
and discussed counseling.
I started to weep,
as the little girl held my hand.

A SECRET HELD
NOT TO DEVASTATE

She walked into class, and the snickering began.
She headed directly for her seat.
The whispers and muffled laughs
danced behind her ears.
She knew what they knew.
The secret she had trusted with her best friend
was not a secret anymore.
It was that evening of open house,
and that night all hell broke loose.
The school's class clown revealed the secret,
that horrible secret.
He announced for the ignoring parents to hear,
including her dear father.
"Yo' pops ain't no accountant.
He's a male prostitute."
She stood embarrassed
as those very words clung to her ears.
She looked for forgiveness in her daddy's eyes,
but he slowly turned around and walked away.

THE IRONY

Smoke filled the sky over the rooftops of houses.

I ran down the street to try to locate the fire.

I started to cough repeatedly from the fumes I inhaled.

My teary eyes saw the blazes exploding from the burning building.

Then there lay a pile of ashes,

where the fire department used to stand.

EARTHQUAKE

Fifteen seconds of horror,
it shook the town.
Crashing glasses and falling roofs,
everyone knew what was going down.
Scurrying people screaming, trying to escape,
but for others, it was already too late.
The bridge had collapsed in a matter of seconds.
How could such a fate happen
on a World Series date?
Now it is time to pick up the pieces,
which everyone seems to say.
But put yourself in their shoes
and see things their way.

IMPLICATED OF A
MINOR OFFENSE

I pushed the cart full of books around the end aisle
purposely to hide from my supervisor.
I came in late to work for the third time,
and I knew what three words faced me.
I peered through the cracks of the shelves
only to spot her lavender skirt coming toward me.
My eyes froze until I heard my name
called in that sturdy voice.

SELF

LIVING WITHOUT LOVE

They say all we think about is love.

We think about it every day.

Wishing for it, dreaming of it,

I must stand alone like usual.

Another love poem,

how sweet.

Another boyfriend,

how nice.

The others are unlike me.

They spend their time being loved.

Being loved, but not cherished,

uncherished by such a foolish young man.

And you ask about my experience with love,

and I will tell you neither.

I have never been loved,

not by a male, nor a female.

MY EYES HAVE SEEN TOO MUCH

I am hoping and praying to whom?
I am begging and pleading not to fall.
I have fought too long not to survive,
in this continuous system.
I cannot go on forever,
with the deterioration of my mind.
Some say they have seen the light.
May I ask what light they have seen?
Because I have not seen any light,
even though I have a victimized mind.
I am not hoping, nor praying anymore,
I have wasted too much time.
No more begs, nor pleads,
it is time for me to say good-bye.

ONE OF THE PRETENDERS

I have led the pretend life too long,
acting so much I have become confused.
I am laughing aloud now,
then crying silently in the bathroom.
I have suffered too long as a nonexistent
and felt the pain as a human.
They say your younger years are the best.
But how can that be
when you don't know who you are?
Why did this soul have to be born,
be born as a nonexistent?
But I am sure when the time comes,
I will have cried my last silent cry.

NOT WANTED AND NOT SEEN

The struggle has become too hard to withstand.
I am crying, not silently anymore.
But why am I alone, without any help?
Do not tell me they cannot see.
Their vision is perfect.
Is it they do not want to see?
View a destroying mind.
I pass them unnoticed,
with a breath of unspoken words exchanged.
Let me say nothing,
although there is nothing to be said.
Let them take part in this ever-dying world.

THE PRETEND LIFE AGAIN

Still leading the pretend life,

I thought it was over.

Until I was taken and shown the normal path,

so I walked it abnormally.

Searching for what I thought was reality.

Hoping for a change,

but I knew everything was the same.

DEAR DIARY:
DESPERATE, MAYBE ...

So I remained silent.

Who can I blame?

I lost my entire self in a way,

I have never lost it before.

Split between two identities that grow yearly.

What happened?

Sex has killed the lost ones, and love ...

It has killed everybody.

Do not learn it,

believe it,

and unwillingly cherish it.

INEXCUSABLE ENCOUNTERS

It slipped away,
like everything else that I knew.
They are the sluts of the world,
taking advantage of my angelic soul,
my pure, clean, and giving soul.
Too pristine for the nature of my character,
and much too evil to conceal the sexual.

AWAKENED TO HAPPENINGS

What happened to my past?
What happened to me?
It did happen to me,
so quickly and so foolishly.
I discovered disbelief,
of something I could not control.
I think I know what happened,
because I have those special eyes.
But sometimes I wonder,
do I know what happened to me?

THE BEAUTY OF DEATH AND ME

Beauty lives on my blood,

draining me of my everyday life.

But I don't worry about it,

because everyone just hands me a knife.

I cry myself to sleep,

no one even knows.

What trouble my mind is in,

when picking out my next-day clothes.

Hopefully, when I die,

no one will cry.

Because when the time comes,

the only tear will be in my eye.

THE BATHROOM

My bathroom is like a dirty, little confession box in a Catholic church.

Where prayers are given and answered for a non-Catholic girl.

Everything is released passionately through masturbation.

God will talk to me, because my soul is discussed daily.

PRESSURES FROM
THE ENVIOUS UNKNOWN

The norms of the world,
The princess of the world,
they conflict naturally.
Therefore, you have to understand
who you are and who I am.

THE SPECIALS

I watch so closely,

viewing what normality cannot.

I was blessed.

By whom?

It.

Can you imagine?

Well, some are just that special,

while others are just that normal.

ONE GOAL, ZERO AMBITION

If I had control of this world,
there would be nothing to unite.

MY SUICIDE

I use to think of suicide as a selfish act.
And the ones who ever thought of
committing this unforgettable crime
held a large amount of ignorance.
Finally, I see what my eyes missed.
I wanted everyone to pay attention to me.
My death scene being played like a vintage film,
all the viewers staring in disbelief
at my bloody, naked body.
They wonder why such an unlikely character
committed suicide.
But they stay uninformed of my mixed emotions.

HIGH SCHOOL:
THE BEST YEARS OF YOUR LIFE

I walked through the hallways.

Figures would go by me as if I did not exist.

Was I different?

Would they try to know me or avoid me?

Electrified by thoughts of being ignored,

it kept my smile in its wrong place.

New faces and old rules,

only in high school.

MY CLASS REUNION

The doors of the gymnasium opened.

The scent of "Class of 1991" came back to me.

Can you believe this school still stands after twenty years?

I see all the '91 students

who back then wanted to be free.

I stay in the corner, hoping not to be recognized.

But it seems impossible,

since I was known as "Miss Lace."

HALF OF ME

Half of me is a bright orange—
shiny and bold
lovely and soft
bursting out of a birthday cake.
But the other side of me is hidden away,
a carnation white, like a flower bud growing—
virgin and pure
new and fresh
dreaming to be a bride of a prince.
Although the two differ,
they both share my soul.

A GLANCE AT SELF

I look over a clustered stack of photographs of me over the years.

I arrange them in chronological order by my ages.

My change of hairstyles,

from pigtails to Mohawks,

makes me think of my childhood,

years in comparison to the present.

My changing body,

broadening mind,

and ever-changing lifestyle

keeps my indentured innocence no secret.

DISAPPEARANCE INTO RELAXATION

The lukewarm water poured into the marble bathtub.

I slipped out of my terrycloth robe.

My feet slid into the warm water, making them tender.

Then my body slinked into the earthy-scented bath.

This small ocean wrapped its slippery waves around me

and massaged me to sleep.

TRILOGY OF ROMANCE

LUST, LOVE, NO, LUST ... LUST ...

The stranger exposed his sensual, magnetic voice.

The voice of a stranger expressed his love for me.

His spicy words floated rapidly into my ears.

My satiny nightgown clung

to my steamy and wet figure.

I answered his fleshy questions in my mind.

My body full of such tangy rawness,

I drifted to his speechless presence.

DO YOU WANT TO TASTE IT?

I lifted the fork to my mouth,
which held the curve-tailed creature.
I placed the well-seasoned shrimp
on the tip of my tongue.
Slowly, I grounded it into small pieces
and swallowed with delight.
My mouth wanted more of the luscious seafood.
Then he sat down at my table,
with his nutmeg brown eyes staring sadly at me,
asking me to share my dinner.
I placed one more shrimp in my mouth,
and as we kissed,
my tongue pushed the tiny entree into his mouth.
I know he truly wanted more.

THE ROMANCE LANGUAGE

He spoke his candid words softly into my ears,
but my failure to understand kept me from responding.
He smiled cleverly as if he knew I misunderstood.
Therefore, silence ruled among us.

TRILOGY OF TRAGEDY

ANGELA'S DILEMMA

It had been raining all afternoon.

So, Angela could not sit in her garden

and look at her blood red roses.

She stared at them from her window,

watching them hang over from the rain.

"They're dying. My beautiful red ones are dying,"

she said to herself.

"I must save them from the angry waters."

She ran outside,

closing the big black door behind her.

She hurried toward the roses

only to fall in the muddy dirt.

Her head facing in front of the dying flowers,

her body did not move,

while the petals of the thirteenth rose dripped with blood.

She died.

But her family need not to dig a grave.

She lay in it now.

MIRANDA'S MURDER

It all began one morning
when he went down to the mailbox
to check how many bills Miranda ran up this month.
But the metal box was empty,
except for this small envelope
in the very back of the mailbox.
He grabbed it and stared at it.
It had no return address,
just "Martin" scribbled on the front.
"Miranda must have done this, but what could it be?"
he thought to himself.
He began to tear open the envelope,
while walking back to the house.
"I hope this is a letter of forgiveness,"
he said to himself.
Miranda waited for him to open the door.
The note read,
"Martin, I forgive you for last night, Miranda."
He smiled, then walked inside the house.
Miranda greeted him
with kisses and silver bullets to warm his heart.

BARBARA'S PROBLEM

She sat at the dinner table,

her eyes gazing up at the ceiling.

"Barbara, you haven't eaten a thing on your plate,"

her husband informed her,

while sitting at the other end of the table.

Her eyes wandered down

until they met with her husband's eyes.

She giggled, and in a childlike voice, answered,

"I took a bite out of this burnt thing that you call a steak."

His face reddened with anger,

"You always have a complaint, don't you? George, I don't
like this, or George, I don't like that."

Tears began to roll off her face.

He did not mean to make her cry,

but she was very sensitive.

He indulged her with apologies and kisses.

She smiled a devious smile.

Night had passed, and morning neared.

The alarm clock rang

to awaken George to a half-empty bed.

"Barb must be fixing breakfast," he thought to himself.

He did not hear

the sounds of pots or any kitchen utensils clanking,

but instead he heard a conversation

going on between his wife and an unknown voice.

Barbara asked, "Do you want eggs with your bacon?"

There was a moment of silence,

and then Barbara replied,

"There's no toast, nor orange juice, but there are muffins and milk. How about that?"

George wondered whom she was talking to.

So, he hurried out of the bedroom

and trekked down the hallway.

He peered over at the dining area

to find his wife sitting at the table,

talking to a plate of food.

What was she … nuts?

George began to walk toward the table,

until her eyes caught a glimpse of her husband.

"I made you breakfast," she implied.

"Who were you talking to just a few minutes ago, Barb?" George questioned.

Her face looked puzzled.

"What are you talking about?" Barbara stammered.

They argued back and forth until

George left late for work.

They argued more than they used to,

but love blinded the truth.

That afternoon came quickly,

and soon, George would be returning.

And where was Barbara?

George came through the front door,

calling out Barbara's name.

She shouted,

"I'm in the bedroom.

I have a surprise for you, darling."

He ran into the bedroom

only to have his heart jump out of his chest.

There she lay on the bed

with that devious smile on her face

and a long silver knife pierced through her heart.

Did he not see her mental illness?

Or did his love blind the truth?

FRIENDS

FOR MY LOST FRIEND

I sing of sorrow and pain,
of the hurt of that horrid day.
Sitting in front of the television,
staring in disbelief
of something too evil, too dark to possibly happen.
You were robbed by death of your graduation,
your prom, and your high school grades—
so young, too young.
I sing of tears,
salty-filled tears at the tip of my lips.
How insensitive of those newscasters
to smile at taken lives.
Of all tragedies I felt or seen before,
none can compare to this unkindly act of fate,
for it has taken part of my soul.

FRIENDS

I talk with my friends every day.

Their different races mean nothing to me.

Black, white, and red claim our contrasting skin tones, but nothing else.

Our special relationship is based on understanding each other, not hatred.

THOSE WERE THE DAYS

She walked through the corridors
crowded with students.
She held her folders and biology book
tightly in her arms.
Her friends waited anxiously at her locker.
They wanted to see
the captain of the football team play.

SMELL THE WEIRDNESS

I awakened from a deep sleep

to inhale the aroma of hearty bacon and gingery cider.

Someone cooked a hot meal.

She made breakfast for me only on special occasions.

I struggled to figure out the date.

Finally, it came to me, October 13th,

nothing spectacular to me.

The savory scent of bacon and cider became burnt.

Then my friend walked in,

holding a platter of crisp bacon,

with a glass of black liquid.

The gaseous stench took me by surprise.

My friend glared down at me,

now holding a silver knife over my chest.

She threatened,

"Friday the 13th just kills me."

I laughed,

but she stayed solemn.

LINDSAY'S GOOD-BYE

Lindsay is the eldest of the three children.

She was packed and ready to go

for her first year of college.

Tears streamed down her face

as she kissed the youngest, Johnny,

and hugged the second youngest, Gabrielle.

She smiled at her parents, and they just looked at her,

as if she was a five-year-old child going to kindergarten.

Lindsay implied, "I'll visit for the holidays."

Her mother nodded,

while her father stood still, looking solemn.

Then her father interrupted the silence,

"Don'tcha make any long distance calls to that
boyfriend of yours. Remember your mother and I pay the
bills."

Lindsay walked slowly out the door,

dismissing her father's words.

She walked toward her boyfriend,

who waited by his car.

She gave him a soft kiss and said in a weak voice,

"Sean, I want you to keep this photograph of me

so you won't forget what I look like."

He caressed her small face and kissed her romantically.
Then, he placed the photo inside his coat pocket.
Lindsay proceeded to her car, not looking back.
She drove down the street
only to disappear in its surroundings.

YOU ARE …

Sweet, sensitive, funny, and generous,
Sister of Blake,
Lover of Alessandrovich, church, and the symphony—
She feels sorrow for the homeless.
She feels great when in love.
She needs family and friends.
She gives joy.
She fears death, loneliness, and the darkness.

NOT SO WOEFUL

MASKING A SENSE OF HUMOR

His brightly colored face and red wig
made the children giggle.
His purple suspenders and baggy pants
made the teens heckle.
His orange socks and floppy shoes
made the adults laugh.
But when the clown left,
the circus filled with complete silence.

FEELING FREEDOM

Its shiny red color attracted me the most.
I ran my hand across the top of the hood
to feel the hot metal.
I even planted a few kisses on its bumper
just to taste its realness.
I jumped behind the furry wheel,
and with a switch of a key, it started.
As the jet black tires began to roll,
I thought of how satisfying it is to have such freedom.

MY SUN

Sunrays are beaming ...
Feel the warmth cover the cold dirt ...
It shimmers and glows ...

HIS COLD

Sneezing and coughing, he reached for a tissue.

"Achoo!"

His wife blessed him.

He muffled a sound of disgust and fell back asleep.

FASHION AND RADIO WAVES HEAD YOUR WAY

Will men wear plastic skirts too?

We have seen the many changes throughout the years.

But now we look ahead to the future of fashion and music.

The break of a strong line of fads and tunes will arrive.

The year 2068 will go down in history.

Styles come in, and styles go out.

Clothes are important to us and always will be.

Silver and gold tones of plastic clothing will be the trend for gentlemen and ladies.

Reusable plastic will be used to create a different outfit every day.

These reusable plastic pieces will be rather expensive.

In addition, the sound of music will definitely change.

Lyrics will discuss topics of the new world.

Different languages will fill our airwaves from Mercury to Pluto.

Robots will be the DJs for your favorite stations,

while you listen to tunes sang by mechanical beings.

So prepare to wear your gold, plastic jeans

and move your feet to the new wave.